Outdoor Play

Val Eustice & Chris Heald

Bright Ideas
for Early Years

Published by Scholastic Publications Ltd,
Villiers House, Clarendon Avenue,
Leamington Spa, Warwickshire
CV32 5PR.

© Val Eustice and Chris Heald

Written by Val Eustice and Chris Heald
Edited by Christine Lee
Sub-edited by Catherine Baker
Designed by Sue Limb
Illustrations by Helen Herbert
Photographs by:
Bob Bray, PP5, 45, 73, 81
John Birdsall, P9
Susan Pitts, P19
John Twinning, PP27, 89
Adrian Rowland, P37
John Kingaby Assocs, P53
Anne Crabbe, P63
Artwork by Norfolk House Graphic
Design Ltd, Leicester
Cover photograph by Martyn Chillmaid
Printed by Loxley Brothers, Sheffield

British Cataloguing in Publication Data
A catalogue record for this book is available from the British
Library

ISBN 0-590-53005-4

Contents

Introduction

For far too many teachers, easy access to outside play facilities is still just a pipe-dream. Schools built in the late nineteenth and early twentieth centuries were designed specifically to block out the slightest view of what was outside and thus avoid 'distracting' the pupils. Many of the classrooms in use for early years children today were designed with the intention of sitting the children at desks in rows, rather than for active learning in play situations, and certainly not to encourage the use of outdoor play space as part of the everyday life of the class.

Access to outdoor play

We want to bring the outside world into the school situation, as a child's learning starts with her own experience of the physical world. Schools are now built so that the pupils can see out of the windows, but there is still a lack of understanding of the need for outdoor access as part of the learning environment for the early years.

With a bit of imagination and internal reorganisation, even the most unpromising classroom can be adapted for explorative active play without too much difficulty. In fact, older buildings often have advantages in terms of space compared to modern ones. It's a different matter where the provision of outdoor play facilities is concerned, as this often has considerable financial implications when it involves (as it usually does) knocking holes in walls and replacing them with doors. Such alterations should be given priority in order to provide good quality early years education.

What is needed?

For satisfactory outdoor play, access to the outside needs to be easy; in other words, you need a door directly to the outdoors from the classroom. A long walk along a corridor to get to an outside door will not seem worth the effort to a busy early years teacher who knows the difficulty of shepherding small children and their tendency to wander or join on to the end of whatever line happens to be passing.

Why outdoor play?

So why do we want children to have access to outdoor play? Why is an adjacent play area not a luxury but an essential?

Many classrooms are small and cramped, so access to outdoor play facilities is a way of making more space available to children for robust play and for larger equipment which is not always appropriate indoors. Moreover, if fresh air and exercise are good for everyone, they must be especially important for the young child at home or at school. To be out in the fresh air under a wide sky gives a sense of freedom and exhilaration and the opportunity to let off steam in a natural way.

Learning by doing

Leaving aside the whole question of playtime and sharing a limited space with a large number of children, outdoor play as an extension of classroom activities encapsulates all the dearly-held beliefs of early years specialists that children learn best by *doing*, by exploring and investigating and solving problems. Even such a simple activity as riding a tricycle down a ramp will involve children in estimating who will go furthest, while a fall of snow can trigger off lots of experiments with slippery ice!

Outdoor play as part of normal classroom practice will help the so-called 'hyperactive' child who has never been encouraged to try to control his movements and is unaware of his effect on surrounding people and objects. Working in a supervised situation with a limited number of children will help such a child gain a measure of self-control, although this will always be a long-term prospect.

In contrast, all teachers will have encountered the child who has never been allowed to play outside and who is anxious and tentative about playtimes. Using outdoor play as a regular extension of classroom activities can help a nervous child overcome his fears.

Supervision

Outdoor play cannot be built into the fabric of class life if children cannot be adequately supervised when they are outdoors. Ideally the teacher should be able to see all of the outdoor play area from any point in the classroom, but if this is not possible, then the children must have suitable supervision. If the only adult in the classroom is the teacher, then outdoor play will be reduced to a large class lesson for a limited period of time, quite divorced from the rest of the school day.

How much better to have groups of children going outside to play at intervals throughout the day, making the outdoors part of an extended classroom! In order to do this, however, a nursery nurse or other trained helper is necessary, and we realise that not all early years teachers have this form of support available. Where such supervision is available, it is not just for the children's safety, but to inspire and motivate them too. Young children need someone to join in their play, suggesting new ideas and ways of doing things and developing and nurturing their emerging skills without 'taking over' and forcing them along paths they have not chosen. Working with young children and developing their play requires a great deal of skill.

Scope for creative play

There are also practical considerations as to why outdoor play should be encouraged. There are some materials such as sand, water, clay and paint which, in the hands of very young children, are very messy indeed. An outdoor area where sand and water can just be brushed away means less wear and tear on the floors and fabric of the classroom. Children need the opportunity to move about freely, to make noise and to make mess, unencumbered by thoughts of what the unfortunate caretaker or cleaner may say on being confronted with a classroom floor awash with water or sand.

About this book

In this book, we have used 'play' in its widest possible sense of 'how children learn', and have included in this definition self-maintaining or 'free' play, play activities which need adult supervision, and play activities which demand some adult input. We have included suggestions for variations and follow-up work which may be possible indoors if your classroom has no outdoor access.

Water play

Chapter one

Water play is one of the most important early learning experiences, and most nurseries and infant classes have access to a water tray of some kind. Children love to experiment with capacity, with pouring, squirting, floating and sinking, and this can be done in perfect safety and at very little cost. Playing with water is not only educational and great fun, but can also be therapeutic and soothing for a child who is upset or nervous. Water play is also a very sociable activity which encourages sharing and talking about what is being done. Added fun can be had by colouring the water with food colouring, but care should be taken that the children's clothes are completely protected by overalls.

When water play is outdoors, there is a greater tolerance of splashes, spills and puddles. Moreover, on a warm day water can be sprinkled about with abandon and will cool everyone down. This freedom to experiment vigorously with water without damaging furniture, walls and floors is what makes water play such an ideal subject for outdoor play.

There's a hole in my bucket

Objective

To allow children to experiment with objects which leak water from different levels, showing how water will only stay in a container up to the level of an outlet.

What you need

Various plastic containers such as bottles and old buckets, nails, a water tray, food colouring, overalls.

What to do

This activity makes the ground surface very wet, and is really only recommended for hot summer days on a tarmac play area.

Use a nail to bore holes into the sides of various plastic containers at different levels, varying the width of the holes. Demonstrate to the children what happens when the bottles are filled (water should squirt from the holes).

Line up the bottles on the ground and let them empty themselves. Let the children experiment to find out which bottle stops leaking first, and which one loses most water.

Ask the children to see if they can keep the bottles full of water. This will keep them busy for a long time until they realise that the only way to keep the bottles full is to block up the holes!

10

Siphoning

Objective

To allow children to discover for themselves the usefulness of tubing for transferring water from one container to another and to introduce the principles of siphoning.

What you need

Lengths of plastic tubing of various thicknesses, a water bath, waterproof aprons, a large water-container of the kind used for camping.

What to do

This is really a very messy activity, so it not only needs to take place outdoors, but also in an area where the water can be sluiced away down a drain.

Let the children experiment with the tubing in the water bath. They will probably just blow bubbles into the water at first, so demonstrate siphoning water into a large water-container, explaining the following points.

● The children should try *not* to swallow the water.

● If the upper end of the siphon comes out of the water, the action stops.

● A thumb over the end of the tube will stop the siphon working.

Painting the town

Objective
To develop hand-eye co-ordination, and to increase awareness of area and, on a warm day, evaporation.

What you need
A brick wall, wooden fence or similar large surface, overalls, buckets of water, wide paintbrushes, powder paint (optional).

What to do
Discuss with the children how decorators use their paintbrushes or what Mum and Dad do when they decorate the house.

Demonstrate the effect of a paintbrush of water on the wall or fence, then let the children take turns to be the painters. On a hot day, the water will dry very quickly. Ask the children if they know where it has gone.

If the fence or wall is not in a position where it is very noticeable, a small amount of powder paint could be put into the water, and the children could then see how long it lasts before it is washed away.

Topsy-turvy

Objective
To encourage children to experiment with the physical properties of air and water.

What you need
A water tray or paddling pool, transparent plastic containers in various shapes, small pieces of card large enough to cover the mouth of the container or thin pieces of plastic or polystyrene from packaging, waterproof overalls.

What to do

This activity is best undertaken on a warm day, perhaps in a paddling pool, as there will inevitably be a lot of spillages.

Allow the children to experiment with the water and the containers. Show them how if they completely fill the tumbler with water, slide a cover on the top and turn it over, the water will not come out. They will then be able to walk about with an upside-down container full of water.

Wishy washy

Objective

To enable the children to appreciate the effect of air and wind on evaporation.

What you need

A bowl of water or a water tray full of warm water, soap, something to wash (for example, doll's clothes, dressing-up clothes or pieces of material from a sample book), waterproof aprons, a washing line, pegs, a laundry basket.

What to do

Suggest to the children that there is some washing to be done, and ask them to decide what they are going to do to get it clean. Talk about washing clothes at home. Who does the washing? How is the washing done; by hand or machine? Why is washing powder or soap added to the water? How is the washing dried? What do you need to do to get the washing dry?

Help the children to organise their washing and their clothes line. They may need some help with pegs at first. Throughout the process, ask the children to describe what they are doing.

Follow-up

● Encourage the children to cut out pictures of clothes from catalogues and stick them on to a drawing of a washing line as a record of their play.
● A trip to a launderette would make an interesting follow-up to this activity.

Sailing along

Objective
To help the children to formulate basic concepts about water as a medium of transport.

What you need
Lengths of plastic guttering with end-pieces (these can be bought at any do-it-yourself shop), waterproof overalls, plastic toy boats, junk oddments which will float such as pieces of wood and foil trays, clockwork boats.

What to do
Assemble the guttering to a length appropriate to your outdoor play area (see Figure 1). Ask the children to help to fill the guttering with water. Place a boat or any item that floats at one end of the guttering and ask the children how they

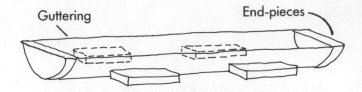

Figure 1

think they could make it travel from one end to the other. Some will push, some will blow, some will make waves in the water. Make sure there are enough 'boats' for everyone who is playing with the water.

Ask questions such as 'How far can your boat go with one push/blow/wave?' or 'Could you put anything on your boat that would make it go faster?'

When the children have had lots of experience with trying to make their boats travel along the water, provide some clockwork boats, so that the children can discover for themselves the difference that a propeller can make.

Car wash

Objective
To allow the children to experiment with the cleaning qualities of water, and to apply knowledge gained at home about washing cars.

What you need
Large outdoor toys such as bikes, scooters, pedal cars and trains, buckets, sponges and cloths, waterproof overalls, washing-up liquid, hosepipe (optional).

What to do
This activity is best done on a warm, sunny day on a hard surface.
 Talk about washing cars and invite the children to wash the bikes and other vehicles in the outdoor play area. Ask questions such as 'Who washes cars?' and 'Why do you think our bikes get dirty?'

Encourage the children to work in groups so that they can exchange ideas and talk freely to each other.

Variation
If you are able to supervise this activity constantly, you might like to set up a hosepipe for rinsing the 'cars'. Be prepared to get very wet!

Fountains

Objective
To allow the children the opportunity to experiment with water pressure in order to develop both their manual dexterity and their understanding of the properties of water.

What you need
Lots of squeezy bottles of various shapes and sizes, a target (possibly pinned to a fence), a water tray or bowls of water, waterproof overalls.

What to do
This is an activity which is great fun outside on a warm day. Ask the children to make the water squirt out of the

bottles. Let them experiment with this before suggesting that they might like to see if they can hit a target with a spray of water.

Ask questions like 'Can you stand farther away and still hit the target?' and 'How far away can you go?' Be sure to show the children how to refill the bottles themselves, and decide on rules about squirting at people.

Develop this play into an experiment by asking the children to stand on an agreed mark and see who can squirt water the furthest, using which bottle.

Treasure cubes

Objective
To provide experience of the meaning of the word 'frozen'.

What you need
Fruit juice, access to a freezer (possibly in the school kitchens), ice-cubes, a variety of containers in which to freeze water, items to put in the ice (for example, beads, novelties from Christmas crackers, large sequins, Christmas cake decorations, buttons and so on).

What to do
Before the activity, prepare some ice-cubes with various small objects frozen inside.

Introduce this activity by giving the children a drink of juice containing ordinary ice-cubes. When the ice-cubes melt, ask the children where they think they have gone.

When they have discussed this thoroughly, get out your prepared ice-cubes and tell the children that there is treasure inside them. Explain that they can see the treasure, but will not be able to touch it until the ice has melted around it. Ask the children to estimate which treasure will be available to them first, and then put the ice-cubes outside, some on the ground, some on a table and some in the water tray. Draw attention to the rate at which the ice melts. Does it melt faster on the ground or in the water?

Follow-up

On subsequent days, provide larger lumps of ice in odd shapes (a wellington boot is fun) and place them around the outdoor play area, in direct sunlight and in the shade, to see which ones melt faster.

Water music

Objective

To develop listening and auditory discrimination skills.

What you need

A water tray or several bowls, waterproof overalls, containers and tools of all kinds, some with lids, some with nozzles, such as plastic bottles with and without tops, squeezy bottles of all sizes, balloons, plastic bags, teapots, jugs, sieves, spoons, whisks, plastic tubing, cones, and so on.

What to do

Ask the children to make as many different noises as they possibly can using the water. Possibilities to explore include:

- slapping the water with a spoon or plastic spade;
- pouring the water from different heights;
- filling balloons with water and dropping them;
- squirting water on to different surfaces;
- putting water inside a container and shaking it;
- putting water inside a container and rolling it along the ground.

Follow-up

Encourage the children to experiment with the different sounds they can make with their bodies:
- slapping hands, legs or cheeks;
- blowing, whistling and hissing;
- hopping, jumping, shuffling and stamping.

Sand and other messy materials

Chapter two

Playing outside with messy materials such as sand, paint and chalk can save a great deal of wear and tear inside the classroom. Of course, we all allow children to use these materials indoors, but the resulting sandpaper effect from sand, the stains from paint and the dust from chalk all restrict the level of exuberance which we can tolerate in a busy classroom.

The same substance used outside in a large open space will encourage a much more light-hearted approach to spills, dribbles and gritty footprints, all of which can be sluiced away. Working with messy materials outdoors inspires experimentation and encourages free expression. The scale of outdoor work can also be much greater, encouraging large movements and life-size models.

Rainbow sand

Objective
To stimulate explorative play.

What you need
Several bowls of dry sand, an empty sand tray, powder paints, wooden spoons.

What to do
Place the bowls of sand around the sand tray and encourage the children to mix a spoonful of powder paint into the sand, using a different colour of paint for each bowl. The sand will change colour, but it will only be very lightly tinted.

When the children have changed the colour in all the bowls of sand, let them choose one and take it to the sand tray. Allow them to add a small amount of water, which will give the sand a much deeper tint. Encourage the children to play with this colour before introducing another. Too many colours will, of course, produce a grubby brown which should be thrown away quickly. A good combination of colours is, of course, yellow and blue which will make the sand green. Encourage the children to play with the different colours. What do they resemble? For example, when the sand is blue the children can pretend it is water, and when it is green the most popular option will probably be grass.

Variations
The coloured sand can also be mixed in heaps on the outdoor play surface in much the same way as concrete is mixed, and then the children can experiment for themselves with colour combinations using handfuls of sand in small bowls.

NB Do not keep this sand for long, since it starts to smell rather musty.

Sandy pictures

Objective
To create a large picture using coloured sand to give an interesting textured appearance.

What you need
Large sheets of paper, such as wallpaper, wrapping paper or lining paper, sand, powder paints, old food containers which have a 'sprinkle and pour' lid (these should be fairly large, as small pepper-shakers do not allow enough sand out for a large picture), sieves, slotted spoons, old squeezy sauce bottles, PVA adhesive, spreaders, glitter (optional).

What to do
Make up some coloured sand as described on page 20. When the sand is dry, pour it into containers with sprinkling and pouring lids.

Help the children to spread PVA adhesive fairly thickly on to the large sheets of paper, and then encourage them to shake coloured sand on to it so that it forms patterns. For example, one child could walk around the edge pouring sand in one colour, and another could sprinkle the centre with patches of another colour.

Variation
Let the children try mixing glitter with their coloured sand and sticking it on to dark paper.

Something cooking in the sandpit

Objective

To allow children to experiment with the moulding properties of sand and to provide an extra dimension to kitchen-play.

What you need

Large amounts of wet and dry sand, either in a sand tray or heaped in a corner or in a sand-pit, pans, baking trays, kettles, wooden spoons, sieves, plates, cups and saucers, jelly moulds, pastry cutters, rolling pins, a table.

What to do

Let the children play in the sand with the cooking utensils, pretending to prepare different sorts of food. Sand is a particularly satisfying material for this kind of play, since it can be mixed and stirred and moulded just like real food.

Take a line for a walk

Objective

To help the children to develop control of their hand and arm movements.

What you need

Rolls of left-over wallpaper, paintbrushes of different widths, empty ice-cream tubs, powder paints of different colours, aprons.

What to do

Mix powder paints with water in wide-necked containers such as ice-cream tubs.

Lay out long pieces of the wallpaper on the ground, blank side up. Ask one child to choose a colour of paint and dip his brush in it. Encourage him to 'take the brush for a walk' along the paper. He can then change his brush and dip it in a different colour of paint, and take it for a different walk along the paper.

Repeat the activity with fresh pieces of paper until every child has had a turn.

Variation

Let each child have one turn of walking with the brush so that each piece of paper becomes a group picture.

Follow-up

Provide chalks, felt-tipped pens of varying thicknesses and smaller pieces of paper in the classroom, and then ask the children if they can take a line for a walk in a new way.

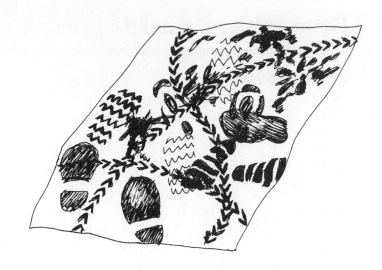

A touch of the Jackson Pollocks

Objective

To show the children that a picture does not need to be painted with a brush, and that attractive patterns can be achieved in other ways.

What you need

Squeezy bottles of paint, spray bottles filled with paint, plastic drinking-straws, old toothbrushes, large sheets of paper, aprons.

What to do

Try the following ideas for creating attractive patterns.

- Put the paper on the floor and let the children experiment with squirting, spraying, blowing and splattering paint all over it. This sort of painting makes a lovely background for smaller pictures and, especially if the colours are limited to shades of red or blue, for example, can really be very expressive of movement.
- Fold a piece of paper in half and ask the children to paint only on one half. Show the children how when they press the blank half of the picture on top of the painted side, they have two matching sides.
- Leave a painting out in the rain. What happens? What does it look like when it dries? Is it still the same?
- Paint the wheels of a tricycle and let the children ride across the paper on it.

Feel free to paint

Objective

To encourage the children to use large arm movements when painting and to encourage free expression with paint.

What you need

A window or fence to which a long piece of paper can be attached, rolls of wallpaper, paint, washing-up liquid, a range of brushes, plastic buckets, aprons.

What to do

Attach a long piece of wallpaper to the fence, then let several children paint on it at once. Encourage them to make big circles on the paper until they are used to the scale, then let them paint a group picture, planning it together.

Variation

Mix some paint with washing-up liquid and let the children paint on the outside of the window.

Impressions of nature

Objective

To use the tactile medium of clay to draw the children's attention to the fascinating patterns and textures which occur in nature.

What you need

Clay (either self-hardening or for firing), an outdoor area with trees, stones and various sorts of surfaces which will leave a pattern on the clay.

What to do

Take the children for a walk around the outdoor play area, pointing out objects with interesting textures and encouraging the children to find other examples.

Encourage the children to make discs or balls of clay, and to press them on to an interesting surface to obtain an impression.

Allow the clay to dry (or fire it if you have access to a kiln). Display the finished impressions on a 'touch table' so that the children can examine the way in which the malleable substance which took the original print has changed into a hard brittle material.

Follow-up

If the clay has been fired, an obvious follow-up would be to 'bake' other substances to see if they also change as dramatically. Include substances which will change, such as eggs, pastry and cheese, but also some which remain the same when put in the oven, such as rice, dried peas and beans.

Silhouettes

Objective

To show the children that chalk-marks on an outdoor surface are not permanent and to encourage them to experiment with the medium.

What you need

Chalks of all sorts (including lump chalk and coloured chalk), toys, at least two sorts of surfaces to draw on (for example, tarmac and paving), cushions or mats.

What to do

Ask some of the children to lie flat on the outdoor play surface, then draw round their outlines with chalk. Do this several times using different colours and thicknesses of chalk, then encourage the children to draw around their friends or the toys.

Over a period of days, point out how the chalk wears or washes away. Talk about which colour vanishes first, and which stays visible longest.

Encourage the children to decide which surface is best for drawing on, then put down some cushions or mats for them to sit on while they experiment with chalk.

Variation

This activity can easily be extended into an experiment to discover which marks last longest, especially if different media are used. For instance, the outlines could be painted over with different substances, for example, powder paint or adhesive, and the most and least permanent discovered.

Wildlife

Chapter three

Most children love to observe and talk about the wildlife they see around them. However, great care must be taken to ensure that the wildlife survives the experience! Small hands can squash and tear without ever meaning to, and children must be taught the correct way to catch and handle reptiles and insects without harming them if they are to interact with their environment in a beneficial way.

The following activities do not fall into the category of free play. They all require an attendant adult to intervene and direct the learning which is taking place, and also to ensure the safety of both children and wildlife.

Equipment such as magnifying viewers and pooters will be useful but not essential, although a magnifying glass of some kind will enhance the children's interest in their observations.

Worming around

Objective
To develop the children's understanding of the importance of worms for the health of the soil.

What you need
A patch of grassy soil, garden fork (optional), plastic containers, a large clear sweet jar, soil, sand, peat, dead leaves, a small amount of well-decayed manure or compost, black paper or cloth.

What to do
Take a group of children to a patch of soil and ask them to jump up and down on it for a while. The vibrations will quickly bring worms to the surface of the soil and the children will enjoy watching them come out of the ground like live spaghetti! An alternative way to obtain worms is to spike the grass with a large fork and waggle the handle; this also makes vibrations in the soil, but is not as much fun to do.

Encourage the children to put the worms gently into plastic containers and observe them closely. Encourage them to talk about what they can see. Ask them what effect they think worms have on the soil. Are worms useful to us?

Put alternate layers of damp soil, peat and sand into a clear sweet jar. Put the dead leaves, compost and worms on the top. Cover the jar with black cloth or paper.

From time to time over the course of a few weeks, take the black cover off your wormery so that the children can see the work the worms have done by moving the layers around and mixing them up.

NB Do not look for worms in deep winter as they hibernate deep in the soil and will not be disturbed by surface vibrations. March to October is the best time.

Bees to honey

Objective
To demonstrate to children the fact that insects are attracted to sweet substances.

What you need
The Giant Jam Sandwich by John Vernon Lord and Janet Burroway (Cape), a sweet liquid such as orange squash, sugar-water or honey-and-water, a savoury substance such as cheese, two unbreakable containers, preferably with a narrow neck.

What to do
Start this activity by reading *The Giant Jam Sandwich* by John Vernon Lord and Janet Burroway.

Put a small amount of a sweet liquid into one container and a savoury substance in another.

Find a place well away from where the children play or sit, where the containers can remain undisturbed.

After a few days, take groups of children to look at the two containers to see which has proved most popular with the insects, and which insects have been attracted.

Obviously this kind of activity has to be done in the warm months when insects are present, although a comparison activity could be done in winter to show the children that there are few insects at this time of year.

Follow-up
• Ask the children to draw a fly as a result of their observations.
• Let them make a large wall-display based on the story of *The Giant Jam Sandwich*.

Incy Wincy spider

Objective
To help the children to appreciate the intricate patterns found in nature, in this case the pattern of a spider's web.

What you need
A place where spiders have spun clear webs (hawthorn bushes are good places to find these, but most bushes will have one or two), a tin of hair lacquer or silver, gold or white spray paint, black card.

What to do
Take the children outside to look for spiders' webs. An autumn morning is a good time for this. When the children have found enough spiders' webs, explain that the spiders have made these webs to catch food, not just as a pattern.

Look carefully around the webs and remove any spiders to a safe place.

Gently spray the web with the paint or lacquer and transfer it on to the card by putting the card underneath it and gently lifting upwards. The paint or lacquer will preserve the web so that the children can look at it more closely.

Follow-up
Talk about the way the spider made the web and ask the children if they think they could make a web too. Ask them to make a web, either by sticking art straws on to paper or by using knitting yarn, which is a little more like the spiders' silk. After they have tried to copy the pattern of a web they will be more aware of the spiders' skill, and will perhaps get a small understanding of the intricacies of nature. Of course, it doesn't matter in the least if the child's 'web' is a bit of a muddle, what matters is the discovery of the spiders' ability.

Going on a bug-hunt

Objective

To show the children how much there is of interest in a small area, and to help them become aware of the minibeasts that remain unnoticed for most of the time.

What you need

Half grapefruit and orange skins, a good reference book on insects, old pieces of wood, logs, containers, large stones, a magnifying glass, drawing materials.

What to do

Prepare the ground for your bug-hunt a good while before the activity, preferably in the winter, so that the insects have the chance to establish themselves in the wood and under the stones. Find a suitable grassy area, preferably near to some bushes, and leave pieces of wood and stones in an out-of-the-way spot.

Very heavy logs and stones which cannot easily be disturbed are best, but a team of workers may be needed to put them in place.

A day or so before your planned bug-hunt, place the half grapefruit and orange rinds around your chosen area. This should ensure that at least you will catch some earwigs! Let the children choose where to put the rinds.

Give each child a container and ask them to find one insect to look at. Stress that they must not fill their containers with all the insects they can find, but they should only ever have one insect in their container at one time and let the others go free.

Whenever anyone finds a different insect, call all the group together to have a look at it.

Insects may only be kept in containers for a short time, but the children can do some quick observational drawings.

Butterfly, butterfly

Objective
To enable the children to understand the life-cycle of the butterfly.

What you need
Cabbage seeds, an area of ground, gardening tools, magnifying glasses, a transparent container, an egg cup, sugar.

What to do
In the spring, let the children prepare an area of ground and plant some cabbage seeds. Leave the young plants unprotected, and eventually cabbage white butterflies will lay their eggs on them. The caterpillars will then feed on the leaves.

Let the children bring leaves with caterpillars indoors to observe closely through magnifying glasses before returning them to the garden.

Watched over a whole summer, the cycle may happen twice. Since these butterflies are very common, you might like to bring a chrysalis indoors and keep it in a container so that the children can observe as it changes into an adult butterfly. Keep an egg cup of sugar-water in the container to ensure that the butterfly, when it emerges, can be fed. This will show the children its curious coiled tongue. The butterfly, once hatched, should of course be released.

Follow-up
Provide the children with appropriate costumes and let them act out the different stages of the butterfly life-cycle. A few small sleeping-bags or sacks make good caterpillars and chrysalides, while net curtains painted with patterns and attached to bracelets at the wrists can lead to a whole flock of 'butterflies' floating around the outdoor play area. A bag of plastic eggs from the role-play shop can be used to represent butterfly eggs.

Water babies

Objective

To show the children the diversity of life to be found in a pond and to foster respect for the environment.

What you need

A pond, large scoop-nets, a bucket of clean tap-water, chlorine reducer (available from tropical fish suppliers), magnifying glasses, wellington boots, old clothes, a reference book with pictures of common pond-life.

What to do

Take the children to look at a nearby pond. Extra adult supervision is essential. Encourage the children to scrape around in the mud at the bottom of the pond with their nets. Help them to lift the nets, as they can be heavy, and drop any small creatures they catch into a bucket of tap-water with a little chlorine reducer added. Let the children look closely at the various creatures through a magnifying glass.

Once they have inspected their catch, encourage the children to put the pond-creatures back into the water as close as possible to the place where they found them.

Follow-up

Let the children make a graph of the creatures they find by drawing each of the species and mounting them on matchboxes next to their own name.

Chick-chick chicken

Objective

To show the children that domesticated animals need lots of care and attention from humans if they are to remain healthy.

What you need

An incubator (you may be able to borrow or hire one of these from your local science advisor), fertile eggs (you may need to contact a poultry-farmer in order to get them), chicken food, bowls for food and water, a chicken pen, a heat lamp to keep the young chicks warm, a cardboard box, plenty of newspaper.

What to do

Before this activity, ensure that you will have good homes for your chickens when you have raised them. This is most important, since you may not want to continue to care for your chickens until they die of old age. We have found it best to hatch the chicks around Easter, care for them through the summer term and hand them over to a good home before the summer holiday begins.

Explain to the children that the incubator acts in the same way as a mother hen's feathers. With the children's help, carefully load the incubator. Explain to the children that they must then wait patiently until the eggs hatch.

Once the eggs have hatched, give each child the chance to hold a chick. Explain that they must be very gentle with them.

Put the chicks in a cardboard box inside the pen, with the heat lamp over them and water and food in a dish. Within a couple of weeks they will be able to go outside in the pen on the grass and the children will be able to scatter their food for them to peck. The chickens can remain outside provided they have wet-weather shelter and are safe from vandals.

There are endless ways of using the experience of seeing chickens hatch and grow to further a child's skills. Very young children can be encouraged to make observational drawings or paintings of the chicks and they can also sequence pictures of their development and investigate what they eat.

Older children could look at the structure of beaks and feet and investigate the insulating properties of feathers.

NB It is not advisable to raise chickens where there are children with allergic airways disease (asthma).

Watch the birdie

Objective

To give the children experience of helping wild birds to survive in the winter.

What you need

A bird-table or a piece of flat ground on which food can be placed, nuts, fruits and berries, breadcrumbs and other leftovers to make a bird-cake, a net of peanuts, bacon rinds, half a coconut.

What to do

Encourage the children to bring food for the birds from home, and organise a rota for going out and replenishing the food on the bird-table during the winter months.

Make a bird-cake using bread, seeds, dried fruit, apple, lard, dog-biscuits, dripping, old biscuits, stale Christmas cake and other suitable leftovers. Put piles of the bird-foods on the table to see which is the birds' favourite food.

Let the children keep a record of the different species of bird which come to the table and ask them to display this information on a chart.

A warm nest

Objective

To show the children how skilful a bird is when making a nest.

What you need

An area of outdoor space where the children can collect material to make a 'nest', plastic bags, round plastic bowls, hay and straw, an old bird's nest, flea-killer.

What to do

Before the activity, dust the bird's nest with flea-killer as birds carry parasites.

Show the children the bird's nest and ask them to look closely at the way in which it was constructed. Talk about the eggs which used to be in the nest, and the adult birds who looked after the young chicks.

Take the children for a walk around the outside play area and ask them to find suitable material for making a nest, letting them choose whatever they feel is appropriate.

Provide plastic bags for each child to carry the materials in if they want, but some children may want to make lots of journeys carrying small amounts like the birds do.

Make the bowls (for use as moulds) and extra hay and straw available, but allow the children to build their nests in their own way, only intervening if they ask for help or are getting very frustrated. Leave the nests in the outdoor play area so that the children can return to them at will. If you do this activity in spring, you will find the nesting materials disappear very fast to make real birds' nests.

Follow-up
Let the children experiment with their materials to make a nest collage, possibly even making a huge picture of a nest big enough for themselves.

A walk on the wild side

Objective
To encourage the children to listen carefully and identify a location by the sounds they hear.

What you need
A tape-recorder and blank cassette.

What to do
Walk around the outside play area collecting sounds and recording them. These could include:

- children playing (the playground);
- bees buzzing (the flowerbeds);
- thumps and bumps (the prefabricated classroom);
- a tractor (the playing field);
- a car door slamming (the car park);
- a bus driving past (the road).

Every outdoor play area will have its own special sounds.

Play the sounds back to the children and ask them where they think each sound comes from. Ask them to give reasons for what they say. There is really no 'wrong' answer, as it depends on the perception of the child and whether they can give a coherent answer.

Variation
- If your school has lots of pets, try recording the noises they make and getting the children to identify them.
- You could also try recording the noises made in different locations in the school, such as the hall, the nursery and the office.

Pathways for play

Chapter four

When teaching young children to understand relationships, it is often concepts of spatial awareness which they find most difficult to understand. The concept 'distance between' does not come naturally to children in their play, drawing or writing — space is there to be filled up.

   If, at seven years of age, children are expected to have grasped such concepts as left and right (something with which many adults have grave difficulties!), we will have to provide opportunities for experiences which build up to this ability, allowing the children to discover for themselves that some way of directing others could be useful, and learning this in a 'pressure-off' play situation. It is our belief that this particular concept is tied to the maturation of the child and should therefore not necessarily be expected of a child at Key Stage 1.

Suggest a winding route around the outdoor play area, something like the route taken by a conga at a party.

This is the sort of play activity to which the children will return many times, inventing different ways of moving around to be copied by their friends.

Copycats

Objective
To develop an awareness of patterns of movement and to encourage taking turns.

What you need
A device for designating the 'leader' (such as a sash, a cuddly toy, a hat or a whistle around the neck), a bicycle or a pram.

What to do
Depending on the confidence of your group of children, you may need to demonstrate this activity a few times!

Let one child be the leader of the group and explain that she should walk or run around the outdoor play area and that the rest of the children should copy her. Let her hold a toy or another item to designate her status as leader. Encourage the leader to invent a different kind of walk, and let everyone else copy it.

Once the leader has had one turn, or at most two, appoint another child as leader, otherwise the more confident children will lead all the time. The idea is for everyone to have a turn.

Once everyone is confident about copying movements like this, introduce the idea of copying a route taken by the leader on a bike or pushing a pram.

Following footprints

Objective

To develop a sense of balance and to provide an opportunity for discovering all the different movements we can make with our feet.

What you need

A stencil of a child-sized footprint, spray enamel paint in two bright colours.

What to do

Before the activity, obtain permission to paint on the playground or outdoor play area.

Taking care to make the gaps short enough for a child-size stride, make a trail of footprints using spray paint and a stencil. This should lead from one side of the play area (not starting just outside the door, as this can cause serious congestion). Do the left and right feet in different colours. Include some large steps, some feet together, some toes pointed in and out, some feet pointing backwards, and so on.

Let the children take turns in following the trail. This should help to develop motor control and encourage concentration.

Variation

Footprints on the outdoor play area could be used as a sort of simple nature-trail to lead children to points of particular interest, such as nesting boxes or buddleia bushes.

Follow-up

• Let the children paint the soles of their feet and the palms of their hands and print with them on to paper. They could make a trail of painted footprints around the walls, and even across the ceiling!

• Let them make trails of hand-prints across the floor, to make it appear as though someone has been walking on their hands. *Orla's Upside-down Day* by M. Smith and J. Lewis (Collins) would be a good story to read with this activity.

• In the summer, let the children make trails of wet footprints which will vanish in the heat of the sun. A paddling pool is ideal for this.

Follow the yellow brick road

Objective
To develop the skills of colour discrimination and balance.

What you need
24 large plastic or wooden bricks (six of each in four colours).

What to do
Arrange the bricks on the outdoor play surface in lines of single colours, placing them a short child-step apart.

Allow the children to choose which colour they want to walk on first, encouraging them to match the name of the colour with the correct bricks. Then let them walk slowly along their chosen line, taking care that they do not overbalance.

For younger children, this activity would be sufficient on its own, but for older children a development would be to mix up the bricks and then let each child choose which colour he is going to step on. This could involve stepping sideways and balancing on one brick while looking for the next one, so it would require a greater level of skill.

Obstacle course

Objective
To encourage the children to design an obstacle course, either verbally or by drawing.

What you need
Suitable equipment to make a simple obstacle course (eg cones, a tunnel, a bench, a box), pencils, paper, mats.

What to do

Ask the children to help you make an obstacle course. Stress that the course is not for racing, but to see how many different ways they can move from one end to the other. Younger children may want to do their planning verbally by discussing which piece of apparatus will go where, although some children may want to draw a plan on paper, showing each piece in the place they want it to go. Whichever way it is done, the plan needs to be worked out to the children's satisfaction. Discuss safety precautions such as mats and turn-taking.

Let the children build their chosen course, then when they have practised on it a few times, ask them if they can think of any improvements or changes they would like to make.

Hansel and Gretel

Objective

To give the children experience of providing as well as following a trail.

What you need

A version of the story of Hansel and Gretel, some light-coloured pebbles, some breadcrumbs, coloured chalks, copies of photocopiable page 94.

What to do

Read the story of Hansel and Gretel, and discuss how Hansel marked the route so that they could find their way back to the cottage.

Take the children outside and let them mark the way back to the classroom using pebbles and breadcrumbs. Use a grassy area if you have one, as pebbles lie better in grass than on tarmac. A few hours later, take the children outside again to see which markers can still be found. Let the children use photocopiable page 94 to record their findings.

Variation

If grass is not available, try using chalk lines instead of pebbles. Each child can then have a colour, so that they can follow their own lines and then go back and follow others. Encourage the children to experiment with their routes, for instance taking them around a post, or up and down a slope.

A good starting point for this activity is *Whistle for Willie* by Ezra Jack Keats (Picture Puffin).

Looking down on things

Objective

To demonstrate to the children that objects seen from above look very different.

What you need

A step-ladder or a large box, everyday items such as a bottle of milk, a cup and saucer, a shoe, a tricycle, a pram, copies of photocopiable page 95.

What to do

This activity needs constant adult supervision. Let the children take turns at standing on a step-ladder or box and looking down from a high vantage point at the outdoor play area. Point out that from this height such things as the tricycle look different, as the wheels are not seen as round, but as straight lines. Show the children a variety of items and let them view them from above. Ask them to describe what they can see.

Follow-up

Let the children look again at the same objects indoors, and see if they can match the top and side views on the photocopiable master on page 95.

Hunt the teddy

Objective

To give the children experience of both giving and receiving clues.

What you need

A small cuddly toy.

What to do

Hide the cuddly toy in the school grounds before the children arrive in the morning. When the children are ready, tell them what you have done, and ask them to look for the toy. When they are close to the toy, tell them that they are 'warm', and when they are far away from the toy, say that they are 'cold'.

Once the toy has been found, let the children experiment with hiding it and telling each other whether they are 'warm' or 'cold'. They will soon find it necessary to ask people to close their eyes or turn their backs so that the toy's

places in the school grounds and ask them to give directions to these places. Record the directions and follow them to the letter. Considerable hilarity can result from this activity, with children quickly reviewing what they have said and producing a revised version.

Variation

Older children who are reasonably fluent writers can try to write directions for their friends to follow, possibly even including instructions on left and right turns.

hiding place is not discovered straight away.

When the children are used to this idea, give them verbal clues such as, 'The teddy-bear is under something green' or 'The teddy bear is on top of something tall', making the clues more and more obvious if they have any difficulty in finding the toy.

Giving directions

Objective

To encourage the children to think about how they would direct others to a specific location.

What you need

Photographs of areas of the school grounds, a tape recorder.

What to do

Talk about the various rooms in the school and ask the children how they would get to each one. Show the children the photographs of the various

Which box?

Objective
To introduce young children to the concept of co-ordinates in a very simple way.

What you need
Chalk in different colours, a doll.

What to do
Before the activity, mark out a nine-square grid on the playground with chalk. Make each row of squares a different colour, and put a circle, a square and a triangle across the bottom. Point out to the children that the boxes on the grid have all got names (green circle, yellow square, etc). Ask if anyone can find the box called red triangle, and ask for a volunteer to stand in it. If this is not forthcoming, use a doll to demonstrate.

Ask each child to make a mark, such as a cross, in a named box with a piece of chalk.

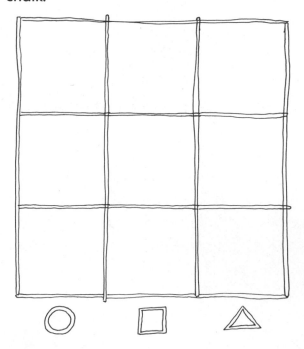

Make a map

Objective
To enable the children to represent their neighbourhood in picture form and understand the basic concept of making a map.

What you need
Car (optional), paint, adhesive, collage materials, brushes, paper for painting.

What to do
Take groups of children for a walk as far as their homes. If this is a long way, using a car might be more appropriate.

On your return, encourage the children to paint a picture of their own house, making details such as curtains by sticking on pieces of material. Talk about who lives near to whom, and introduce the concepts of maps and relative distance. Ask them if they could make a map of their area. What street names will they need to include on their map? It will probably be necessary for you to provide a background framework of roads, since young children tend to have difficulties with spatial relationships, but allow the children to design their own map as far as their skills will allow.

Running, jumping, standing still

Chapter five

Running around in the fresh air in the summertime has to be counted as one of the great joys of childhood. It offers the opportunity to burn off excess energy and to stretch muscles in a way that is not always possible indoors. Young children need to have lots of 'free' outside play, but they can also benefit from a more formal activity which explores a particular skill such as walking on tip-toe or jumping. The following activities are all simple games with simple rules.

Find your colour

Objective

To enable the children to form small groups quickly and easily, and to reinforce knowledge of colours.

What you need

Four plastic cones, hoops or PE baskets of different colours, badges, bands or tabards in the same colours, a whistle.

What to do

Put the four coloured objects in different parts of the outdoor play area. Point out the match between the colours of the objects and the children's badges, tabards or bands.

Tell the children that they can run around the outdoor play area until they hear the whistle, at which point they should return to their own colour 'base'.

Once the children have done this several times and can find their colour every time, introduce the idea of being first back to the base. Alternatively, with older children, ask them to exchange bands during the 'runaround' period, so that their base will be constantly changing.

Roll over

Objective

To develop the idea of taking turns, and to have a great deal of fun in the process.

What you need

A long gentle grassy slope, two or more noise 'signals' such as swannee whistles, castanets and bells.

What to do

Encourage the children to experiment with rolling down the slope. If they have never done this before, they will need

plenty of time to play and get used to the idea!

When the children have exhausted the novelty of the idea, introduce the signal noises, explaining that when they hear the castanets, they should jump up and down, and when they hear the whistle, they should roll down the slope. Allow the children to take turns making the noises with whistles and castanets.

This activity can, of course, be done on a flat area, although it is not nearly as much fun, and requires much more effort to roll.

Variation

If space is restricted, divide the children into groups, saying that one group can only roll down the slope when the whistle blows, and the other group can only roll when they hear the castanets. With very young children the activity would probably be more successful if done with a smaller group.

Keep your balance

Objective

To encourage children to develop their sense of balance in a play situation.

What you need

Several long skipping ropes, bean-bags.

What to do

Before the activity, arrange the skipping ropes in different patterns around the playground, as in Figure 1. Encourage the children to walk carefully along the skipping ropes, like a tight-rope walker. Show them how they can use their arms for balance.

When the children become adept at this, let them try to do the same thing with a bean-bag balanced on their heads. It's amazing how difficult it then becomes, since they can't look at their feet without losing their bean-bag!

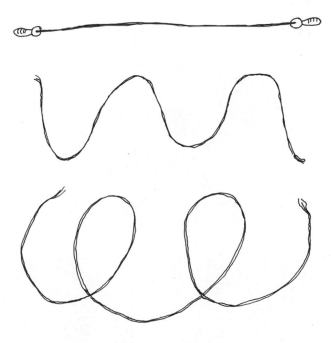

Figure 1

Ring games

Objective
To encourage co-operative play and to match actions to a rhyme.

What you need
No special equipment.

What to do
Sing the rhyme and do the actions to a well-known ring game such as 'Ring-a-roses', 'The farmer's in his den', or 'There was a princess long ago'. The following example should be sung to the tune of 'Here we go gathering nuts in May' and aims to foster co-operative play.

What shall we do in the playground
    today, playground today, playground
    today,
What shall we do in the playground
    today,
That we can do together?
We can clap hands in the playground
    today, playground today,
    playground today,
We can clap hands in the playground
    today,
And we can do this together.
We can stamp feet . . .
We can jump up . . .
We can sit/fall down . . .
We can turn round . . .
We can hold hands . . .
© C. Heald, 1990.

Ask the children if they can think of any other actions that everyone would be able to do, and add these to the song.

Young children will need lots of practice before they develop enough control to stand completely still, so it should be accepted as an appropriate response if they stop running and stand more-or-less on one spot.

Once the game is understood by the children, introduce running on tip-toe, hopping, jumping, etc. Let the children take turns to blow the whistle.

Stepping stones

Objective
To encourage the children to develop the ability to stride or jump.

What you need
Six hoops.

What to do
Before the activity, arrange the hoops on the ground so that the children can jump

Freeze!

Objective
To develop listening skills and gross motor control.

What you need
A whistle.

What to do
Explain to the children that you are going to ask them to run about, and that then you will blow the whistle, at which point they must freeze and stand very still.

between them. Encourage the children to stride or jump from one hoop to the next without stepping outside the hoops. With older children, place the hoops further apart and use the context of 'islands', with some children designated as 'sharks' in the waters between, waiting to carry off the travellers who step off between the hoops. This might, however, cause some distress occasionally for nursery or reception children.

Variation

● Instead of a single pathway, just have an area of hoops with different spaces between them, and allow the children to pick their own pathway across. The distance between the hoops can then be increased as the children become more confident about striding or jumping across the spaces.

● Another alternative would be for the children to crawl through the hoops, lifting them over their heads before moving on to the next one. This could be done using a sequence of colours, in which a child might have to move from a red hoop to a yellow one, and so on.

Jumping beans

Objective

To encourage children to think of lots of different ways in which to jump.

What you need

Several different sound 'signals', such as a whistle, a tambourine and castanets.

What to do

Start by asking the children to take little jumps, then ask for big jumps. Move on to jumping from side to side and from front to back. Be prepared to join in and demonstrate! Ask if the children can jump on one leg (ie hop).

Let the children rest while they think about all the different ways in which animals can jump. These could include:
• a kangaroo leaping on two strong back legs;
• a rabbit stretching his front paws out in front and bringing his hind feet up to meet them;
• a frog with his front legs held between his back legs.

Tell the children that you will be using a different sound to denote each animal. Then, for as long as a particular sound is being made, the children should jump like that animal.

This can be a very tiring activity, and should only be done for a short while.

Pass the daisy

Objective

To provide the opportunity to perform an action which is structured by the game and therefore not too threatening for a young child.

What you need

No special equipment.

What to do

Take the children out to the playing field on a dry, warm day and ask them to sit down in a ring. Teach them the following rhyme, which is sung to the tune of 'London Bridge is falling down'.

Here's a daisy, pass it on, pass it on, pass it on,
Here's a daisy, pass it on, I'll give it to my friend.

(Spoken) It's not for you, it's not for you,
it's not for you, it's for YOU!
© C. Heald, 1990.

Let one child pick a daisy, and ask her
to pass it round the ring while the
children sing the song. Tell the person
who is holding the daisy on the last
'YOU!' that they should stand up and
choose a friend to give the daisy to. The
friend should then change places with the
daisy-holder and send the daisy on its
way again.

This activity can, of course, be done
with a bean-bag or something of that
nature, but a flower is a natural present
for a young child to give, and since they
are usually in plentiful supply in the
summertime, there shouldn't be much
difficulty in obtaining some.

Follow-up

This game can lead on to the more
competitive 'I wrote a letter to my love'.

Let's pretend

Chapter six

It is generally accepted that role-play is an essential learning activity for young children. Not only does it provide a stimulating and exciting environment for language development, it also encourages children to mix socially and promotes sharing skills.

The children also have the opportunity to re-create real experiences actively and thereby make sense and give meaning to the world around them.

Most early years classrooms provide a role-play area within the school building, but there is more scope for realism and for messy activities in outdoor play. Many role-play situations demand an outdoor atmosphere and sufficient space for movement which can only be provided outside the classroom.

Many of the following activities could be initiated by a visit to a real location, and we have found local businesses and factories most welcoming and accommodating.

The seaside

Objective

To provide tactile experiences of sand and water in a realistic environment.

What you need

Holiday snapshots and postcards showing beach scenes, plastic sheeting or a heavy duty groundsheet, a large quantity of sand, a paddling pool or baby bath of water, blue food colouring, a variety of props and clothing to create a seaside atmosphere (this could include shells, buckets and spades, fishing nets, towels, pretend fish made from thin slices of carrot, flippers, snorkels, surfboards, rubber rings, beach balls, sunglasses, sun hats, empty sun-cream containers).

What to do

Begin with a visit to the seaside if possible, but if this is impossible, discuss the children's own experiences of the seaside. Use holiday snapshots, postcards and stories about the seaside to stimulate the children.

Reconstruct a seaside scene in the outdoor play area, with sand on plastic sheeting and a paddling pool filled with water dyed blue with food colouring. Adult supervision is advisable at first, to guide the children through safe play. For example, children should know that sand is best kept on the plastic sheet, that they can only paddle on a warm day, and so on.

Ask questions to draw the children's attention to related subject areas. For example:

- Can you build a tall sandcastle?
- How many fish can you catch in your net?
- What would happen to real fish if you took them out of the water?

Follow-up

- A sound effect tape could be used to add to the seaside atmosphere and stimulate discussions.
- Transport such as toy cars could be used to travel from the classroom to the 'seaside';
- Ice-lollies and ice-cream could be made in class to extend the seaside theme.
- The opportunities for related art work are endless.

Ship ahoy!

Objective

To enarge the children's experience of boat rides and possible connected leisure activities.

What you need

The loan of a real boat (a small rowing boat fixed in a safe position in the playground would be ideal) or a modified construction of boxes or a disguised climbing frame, a collection of objects to extend the authenticity such as a large cloth sail and a variety of flags, a selection of life jackets (baby swimming-floats are ideal), toy fishing rods and nets.

What to do

A possible introduction to this activity would be through water play. The discovery of things that float could lead to an examination of different types of boats, such as barges, dinghies or rafts. If a paddling pool and small dinghy are available, the children can experience the sensation of floating. For obvious reasons, supervision is essential when the paddling pool is used. Toy fishing rods and nets can also be provided, and the children could play at stormy days, shipwrecks and so on in the pretend boat.

Follow-up

The children could make their own magnetic fishing game using card fish with paper-clips attached, and small fishing rods made from garden canes with small magnets fastened to the string.

Santa's grotto

Objective
To create a fantasy situation which is extremely exciting and magical for young children.

What you need
A climbing frame, a large sheet, spray snow, glitter, adhesive, a large cardboard box, scissors, paints, brushes, a selection of wrapped boxed parcels, costumes for Santa, reindeer, elves and fairies.

What to do
This is an activity for the period just before Christmas, when the weather will be very cold for outdoor play. However, do not let this put you off — it is a very valuable experience for children to play out this fantasy. Our nursery found it a very rewarding role-play experience. The stimulus was the festive season and the school Christmas production. The costumes and props from the play were 'borrowed' for two weeks and the children continuously acted out the magic of Christmas. They sang all the popular songs, and some days it was so cold that everyone ended up with red noses — not just Rudolph!

Let the children help you design 'Santa's grotto'. This can be done by draping a large sheet over a climbing frame and decorating it with glitter or spray snow. Encourage the children to be imaginative in their designs.

Cut away the flaps and one end of a large cardboard box and let the children decorate it as a sleigh. Arrange the presents and the sleigh around the grotto and let the children act out the roles of Santa Claus and his attendants.

The potting shed

Objective

To design an instant garden without a frustrating wait for the real growth cycle.

What you need

A variety of pot plants, planting troughs and tubs, grow-bags, small garden tools, a wheelbarrow, seeds, watering cans, garden gnomes, artificial grass, plastic flowers or homemade paper blooms.

What to do

Introduce the theme by taking the children for a walk down local streets to look at gardens. Draw the children's attention to the grass, trees and flowers.

Re-create a garden in the outdoor play area using artificial plants, pot plants and garden tools. Allow the children to play in the designated area, experimenting with different arrangements of artificial flowers and grass.

Growing real seeds, of course, takes longer. Let the children grow cress and marigolds, as these germinate quickly, so the children will soon see results. The children might also like to grow sunflowers, which are exciting plants to grow, but they do take much longer.

Follow-up

A natural extension of this activity would be an examination of the conditions necessary for growth. An experiment could be set up where three pots of seedlings are grown in different situations. For example:

- pot 1 — without water or light;
- pot 2 — without light;
- pot 3 — with water and light.

The results can be examined and discussed.

Pavement café

Objective

To give children experience of exchanging cash for goods and services.

What you need

Large table, cakes, sandwiches and rolls made from safe unbreakable substances such as foam rubber or card, small tables and chairs, toy money, till, dressing-up clothes, a collection of props.

What to do

Discuss the children's own experiences of eating out, then set up a pavement café in the outdoor play area with tables and chairs, imitation food and toy money. Let the children assume the roles of customers and waiters. Try to ensure that the children take turns at serving; usually they all want this role. Vary the roles of customers by providing various props, such as dolls and prams, policeman and fireman outfits, to enrich play. Try to change the types of food available, as young children will quickly get bored with using the same resources and the quality of play will deteriorate.

The garage

Objective

To develop an understanding of basic technology and to demonstrate that a system must be correctly assembled in order to work effectively.

What you need

A variety of toy cars, some made from construction kits (for example Gymbo, which can be broken down and then reassembled), toy telephone, notebook, collection of car mechanics' tools (either real or toys), foot-pump, jack, battery charger, empty oil cans, overalls, crash helmets, large cardboard boxes, paint, brushes, rubber tubing, buckets, sponges, a car.

What to do

Start the activity with a discussion about cars, and follow this up by allowing the children to look at a car. Let them look under the bonnet. They will be particularly fascinated by the engine.

Continue the theme by helping older children to organise a car wash service for the staff. This can then be followed up by a visit to a local garage with a car wash facility.

Finally, let the children set up their own 'garage' in the outdoor play area. Encourage them to make petrol pumps, both leaded and unleaded, by painting cardboard boxes and attaching lengths of rubber tubing. Let them use the toy cars, tools and other props, including a toy telephone and notebook for appointments.

Allow the children to dismantle the cars made from construction kits, and then ask them to reassemble them so that they work properly.

Follow-up

A short topic on road safety could easily be linked with this aspect of role-play. Visits to the classroom by a policeman or lollipop lady would lend reality and stimulus to this work.

Wild West

Objective
To develop the children's awareness of different lifestyles and cultures.

What you need
Tepee tents (either commercially produced or a simple homemade construction), a variety of fringed costumes, feathered headbands and cowboy outfits, face paints, baby lotion, non-toxic fluorescent paint, rocking horses or hobby horses, books and videos about American Indians.

What to do
Introduce the topic through stories, rhymes and videos. Make the children aware that people around the world live in different types of homes, depending on weather, lifestyles, and so on.

Let the children use role-play to explore the traditional lifestyle of American Indians. Help them to understand that what they have seen on television might not necessarily reflect reality.

Let the children experiment with face paints to enhance their costumes. Baby lotion mixed with a small amount of non-toxic fluorescent paint makes a spectacular face paint which is both easy to remove and does not seem to irritate the skin. However, we would suggest that parents' permission is sought before using this.

There are several simple songs which could be used to motivate children in their role-play, such as 'Land of the silver birch' or 'We are the Red men'.

Follow-up
Different types of homes could be investigated, starting with the children's own houses. Ask questions such as:
- What is your house made of?
- Does it have a sloped roof? Why?
- Why do we have windows?

Fairy castle

Objective

To develop fantasy play in an exciting realistic environment.

What you need

A cover which can quickly transform the climbing frame into a castle, such as pieces of silver or gold foil attached to old sheets, corrugated cardboard, silver or gold spray paint, a selection of dressing-up clothes, rocking horses.

What to do

Introduce this theme by using several fairy stories to motivate the children. Suitable stories would be Sleeping Beauty, Cinderella, Jack and the Beanstalk and Snow White.

Create a fairy castle by covering the climbing frame with sheeting decorated with foil, and make turrets by spraying corrugated cardboard silver or gold and bending it into the appropriate shape.

The children could then experiment with the castle. Use it as the scene for storytelling, with the children dressing up and acting out the storyline. Then encourage them to develop their own storylines. This is important, as without this the role-play could quickly become based on a playhouse situation.

Health studio

Objective

To explore the value of physical exercise and general fitness.

What you need

A variety of PE equipment, mats, appropriate costumes (leotards, shorts, sweatbands, wristbands, baseball caps), a toy telephone and appointments book, a battery-operated tape recorder, fitness cassette tapes, a keep-fit video.

What to do

Discuss the importance of keeping strong and fit through exercise. Are any of the children's parents involved in fitness programmes? What do they do? What equipment do they use? Show the class a short excerpt from a commercial keep-fit video tape. Encourage the children to discuss what they see.

Let the children set up their own 'health studio' in the outdoor play area. Ensure that a soft landing is provided and that adequate staff supervision is always available. Let the children take on the roles of studio staff and customers. Encourage the studio staff to make up fitness programmes for their customers to follow.

The builder's yard

Objective

To show how different materials have a variety of properties.

What you need

A visit to a building site, old bricks, sand, water, small planks of wood, a variety of old tools, overalls, toy wheelbarrows.

What to do

Organise a visit to a building site or any form of new construction while building is in progress. A home extension at a pupil's house would be ideal. Draw the children's attention to ways of arranging bricks to form strong bonds. Let them watch while cement is mixed, and compare this to the adhesives the children have used.

Set aside a part of the outdoor play area as a builder's yard and allow the children to experiment with building materials. Direct their work towards 'long' walls, 'high' walls, 'thick' walls, and so on. Our children constructed their own small wall three years ago and, much to our amazement, it is still standing!

To extend the work, our four-year-olds took the story of Humpty Dumpty, and using a paper egg cut into three pieces, explored the adhesive qualities of various sticky substances. They tested commercial adhesives, jam and wallpaper paste in their attempts to stick him back together. The jam showed good short term results!

The weather

Chapter seven

The links with the weather in the following activities will be easily recognised by the children. We have tried to outline some activities which will encourage them to investigate and discuss both the properties and the consequences of weather changes.

It is important that the children are suitably dressed for the planned sessions, and therefore parental support must be enlisted to send the children to school with the required outdoor footwear and waterproof clothing.

We found that some of our children were quite reluctant to venture outside in cold or wet weather, and lots of encouragement and motivation were needed. However, once one or two intrepid children were enticed outside, the others quickly followed.

Ice is nice

Objective
To give experience of water in its frozen state.

What you need
Rubber gloves, a refrigerator, food colouring, bowls, balloons, a variety of plastic moulds.

What to do
Take the children outside on a very cold day to look at frozen puddles and icicles.

Draw the children's attention to the different shapes of the ice.

Bring some ice inside and allow it to melt. Encourage the children to touch the smooth, hard, shiny surface of the ice and compare this to the feel of water.

Talk about making ice-cubes and ice-lollies in the freezing compartment of the fridge, and then experiment with making ice in different shapes and different colours by adding a small amount of food colouring.

Rubber gloves filled with water and then tightly tied make fascinating frozen shapes, as do balloons of different shapes. Once removed from the moulds, these shapes can then be allowed to melt in bowls around the classroom. Alternatively, let the children play with them in the water tray. Warn the children that the ice might stick to their skin if they hold it for too long.

Let the children explore various locations, in and around the school, to see where ice melts most slowly. Hopefully they will suggest that the radiator is not a good place for this but that the playground would be.

Footprints in the snow

Objective
To examine the properties of snow and to investigate and match footprints.

What you need
Powder paint in shallow trays, saucers, magnifying glasses, children's wellington boots, old cloth, coloured bricks.

What to do
When there has been quite a heavy snowfall, ask the children to bring wellington boots to school for outside play. Let them enjoy free play, exploring the sticking and moulding properties of snow. Let them hold small pieces of snow and watch it melt. Explain that this is due to body heat. Small saucers of snow can be examined with magnifying glasses to look at individual snowflake designs.

Limit the free play to a small section of the playground, so that the remaining smooth surface of snow can be used for experiments with footprints. To make these more interesting, let the children first step into a tray of dry powder paint and then create coloured footprints in the snow. The colours will highlight the patterns on the soles of the boots.

Create simple treasure hunts by burying a red brick in the snow at the end of a trail of red footprints and a blue brick at the end of a trail of blue footprints, and so on. The snow should clean most of the paint from the boots, but have an old cloth available to wipe them completely clean, or trails of coloured footprints could be made throughout the classroom.

Follow-up
The children could look at animal prints in the snow and try printing with doll's shoes on white paper to recreate their experience.

What colour is rain?

Objective
To examine the pollution in the air and investigate some separation processes.

What you need
Clear plastic containers, funnels, magnifying glasses, pebbles, dried peas, tea leaves, filter papers, a selection of sieves and collanders.

What to do
Watch the rain falling outside. Discuss what colour the children think it is. The replies from our nursery children were very surprising.

Collect the rainwater in plastic containers, and then bring it in and examine it, first with naked eyes and then with a magnifying glass. You may be surprised how dirty it is. Ask the children where they think the dirt comes from.

Practise various separation processes using combinations of pebbles and water, dried peas and water, tea leaves and water, poured through a variety of sieves and tea-strainers. Suggest to the children that sometimes particles are so small that they need a special strainer, ie filter paper in a funnel, to separate them from water.

Follow-up
• Investigate cleaning materials such as soap, detergent and washing-up liquid.
• Draw the children's attention to the different properties of hot and cold water and soap in a controlled experiment on greasy plates or dirty sinks.
• Discuss pollution in simple terms with the children. Look at household and factory chimneys and car or lorry exhaust pipes. It is generally possible to develop an awareness of the need to care for the environment, no matter how young the pupils are.

Keep our gnomes dry

Objective
To discover which materials are waterproof.

What you need
Umbrellas, plastic sheeting, tin foil, tissue paper, newspaper, art paper, plastic beakers, elastic bands, plastic drinking straws or Constructo-straws, a garden gnome.

What to do
Before the activity, place the garden gnome in the outdoor play area.

Take the children out in the rain with umbrellas so that they can observe how the umbrellas keep them dry. Let them look at the strategically placed garden gnome and discuss how their umbrellas are too big for him. Set the task of designing an umbrella of the right size which will keep the gnome dry.

Get the children to test various materials by covering beakers with samples of each and securing them firmly with elastic bands. Place the beakers out in the rain, ensuring that the children understand that you want to find a material which can keep rain out of the cup.

After an agreed period of time, examine the results of the experiment and let the children select an appropriate material with which to make their umbrella. Explain that the umbrella does not have to be a traditional circular shape. Straws could be linked in square or triangular shapes, and then covered with the chosen material. The children may find the construction of the umbrellas difficult, but teacher assistance is valid as the important issues are the concept and investigation.

Follow-up
Look at constructions which allow rain water to drain away, such as sloping roof shapes, tents, guttering, etc.

Puddle play

Objective
To observe water movements.

What you need
Wellington boots, raincoats, pebbles, lolly sticks, oil-based inks, a water tray, a hairdrier, paper.

What to do
On a rainy day, allow the children to put on waterproof clothing and go into the playground to look for puddles. Encourage them to look carefully at the water surface.

If it is raining, ask the children to watch the patterns of concentric circles made by large raindrops. If it has stopped raining, let them look at the smooth surface and then drop pebbles in. Push lolly sticks across the surface to demonstrate the 'V' shaped ripples created on the surface. Ask the children to blow across the surface of the water and make parallel wave-like patterns.

Back in the classroom, try to recreate and capture these patterns using oil-based inks floated on trays of water. Allow the children to drop in a pebble, and then quickly take a paper print of the resulting surface patterns. A hairdrier may also be used to create wave patterns to be captured on the paper.

Follow-up
Together with the children, watch raindrops running down the window pane. Recreate these with syringes of water-based paint squirted on to paper stuck on a window. The children can watch the patterns the paint makes as it runs downwards, but don't forget to place lots of newspaper on the floor to collect the resulting puddles.

Summer scorcher

Objective
To investigate the changes produced in substances melting in the heat of the sun.

What you need
Assortment of foods which will melt when exposed to sunshine, such as ice-cream, chocolate, butter, ice-lollies and jelly, paper.

Human sun-dials

Objective
To investigate shadows and the movement of the earth around the sun.

What you need
Coloured chalk.

What to do
Take the children outside first thing on a sunny morning to look at their shadows on the playground surface. Allow them to experiment with making different types of shadow. If there is a shaded area in the playground, let the children enter it and make their shadows disappear. Talk about what makes shadows and how our bodies block the sun's rays thus creating a silhouette outline.

What to do
Examine the food with the children and ask them what they think will happen to it if it is placed in the sunshine. Encourage the use of words such as melt, solid and liquid. Place the materials out in a sunny spot and periodically check what is happening. Ask the children to rank the substances in order of the speed with which they melted. Make sure the children understand that it is the *heat* from the sun which causes this melting action, not the light.

Ask the children what could be done to try to restore the solidity of the materials. Many children will suggest putting them in the fridge. Would this return the substances to their original form? Let the children make melted pictures from different coloured chocolate and butter, by leaving the substances to melt on a piece of paper, then scratching and swirling them into a pattern. Leave the patterns in a cooler place to solidify.

Choose a child to be a model. First draw round his feet with the chalk on the playground surface, then draw round his shadow. Record his shadow in different coloured chalks at various times throughout the day, always ensuring that his feet are placed inside the original footprint outlines. This will produce a circle of shadows indicating the movement of the earth in relation to the sun. This concept is most difficult for young children to grasp as they always assume that it is only the sun which has moved!

Follow-up

There are many further activities which can be done with shadows, such as making hand shadow shapes, card shadow puppets and cameo cut-outs in black paper, and playing shadow matching.

Dry the washing

Objective

To investigate how the wind aids the evaporation process.

What you need

Two washing lines (one in a sunny, windy location and the other in a sheltered, shady spot), dolls clothes, bowls, washing powder (some children may be allergic to biological washing powder, so parents' permission should be sought first), clothes pegs.

What to do

Take a selection of doll's clothes outside to wash in warm soapy water. Encourage plenty of discussion during the washing process by asking questions such as:
• Why do we use soap?
• Why use warm water?
• Who washes your clothes? How do they do it?

Once clothes are washed and rinsed, ask the children to choose one of the washing lines on which to hang the clothes to dry. Throughout the day, keep testing the clothes to see if they are dry. Hopefully the clothes exposed to both sun and wind will dry more quickly than the others.

Follow-up
Wash two dolls' hair and then ask the children which will dry quicker — one left to dry alone or one which is dried with a hairdrier. After the predictions, test the theories using a hairdrier.

Mrs Mopple's *Washing Line* by Anita Hewett (Bodley Head/Puffin) is a perfect story to illustrate the concept of a drying wind.

Wind direction

Objective
To observe the variety of wind movements.

What you need
A collection of objects which indicate wind direction, such as flags, balloons on string, kites, bubbles and streamers, thin plastic sheeting, scissors, canes, cotton.

What you do
Take the children out on to the playground on a windy day and draw their attention to the direction in which grass, trees and chimney smoke are

blowing. When discussing direction use easily recognisable landmarks, such as 'the wind is blowing towards the street', and so on. Show the children a collection of things which could be used to show the direction of the wind, such as flags, balloons, kites, bubbles and streamers. Balloons are particularly good fun, and make a good indicator of wind direction. However, the favourite in our school is most definitely bubbles. The children love watching which way they blow and enjoy catching and bursting them.

Ask the children to make their own simple flags or kites using lightweight materials such as thin plastic sheeting or thin cotton attached to canes. These can then be taken outside and held up to discover wind direction.

Follow-up

Follow-up activities could include bubble printing and blow painting through straws.

Games in the playground

Chapter eight

This chapter suggests games and play situations which require painted areas, either on the playground or on the surrounding outside walls. These painted outlines provide opportunities for children to play fantasy games or practise hopping and ball games without tedious preparation on the teacher's part.

It is important not to crowd the playground with too many of these painted areas, or else it will be overpowering and will fail to stimulate the children. Similarly, it is advisable to change the outlines at least twice a year to avoid the children becoming bored and consequently ignoring the designs.

We are lucky in that our Local Education Authority provides us with painted playground areas, and the painters update and modify the designs twice a year. However, if this service is not available to you, the only requirements are a sympathetic headteacher and governors and some gloss paint.

Colour hopscotch

Objective
To introduce the children to a simplified game with established rules and patterns.

What you need
Paint and brushes or chalk, coloured bricks or discs.

What to do
If you want to try the effectiveness of this activity without the permanence of painting, chalk an outline on the playground initially. Use blocks of colour instead of numbers. We would suggest using simple basic colours at first, such as red, blue, green, yellow, white and black. It is also a good idea to limit the number of squares in the grid.

Hopscotch is subject to regional variations, so if you are unsure of the basic outline and the rules, it might be advisable to undertake this activity with the help and advice of an older class of children. Their teacher might even like to set them the task of devising a hopscotch grid for young children.

Show the children how to jump with their feet apart and also how to hop on one foot. Before introducing the rules of the game, let the children experiment with hopscotch jumping in the outline.

When this has been sufficiently mastered, introduce coloured bricks or discs for the children to match up with the coloured squares as the format of the hopscotch game is developed. This provides a multi-skill game involving throwing with accuracy, hopping, jumping and colour matching.

Follow-up
Later, as the children grow more proficient, extra squares can be added to extend the hopscotch grid and more complicated colours can be used, such as turquoise, lilac, maroon and pink.

Amazing mazes

Objective

To promote visual discrimination and to encourage the children to consider the consequences of their actions in order to negotiate a maze successfully.

What you need

Paint and brushes or chalk, plastic shapes or numbers, copies of photocopiable page 96.

What to do

Using Figure 1 for reference, paint or chalk a maze in the playground, with home bases in the corners displaying shapes or numbers of your choice for matching or recognition purposes.

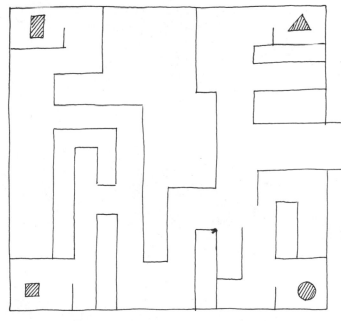

Figure 1

Explain the concept of a maze to the children, and stress that they are not allowed to cross over the lines. Adult supervision will be necessary until the children are used to such disciplines, otherwise they may simply run from

corner to corner treating the game as a race. Once the children have mastered keeping to the pathway, many additional learning experiences can be introduced.

• Give the children a plastic shape or a number and ask them to match it with the appropriate corner, walking successfully through the maze.

• Ask the children to respond to a verbal command such as, 'Go to the triangle corner please, Nicola'.

• Encourage the children to translate these directional skills into pencil exercises using photocopiable page 96.

The schoolyard express

Objective

To encourage controlled movements in a specific direction around a designated pathway.

What you need

Chalks or paints and brushes, a visit to a local railway station.

What to do

A visit to the local railway station followed by general discussion about a train journey would be an excellent introduction to this activity.

Paint or chalk on the playground an outline of a railway track curving round in a continuous cycle, with various stopping places marked around the track, as in Figure 1.

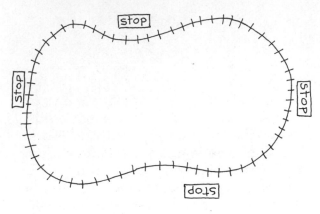

Figure 1

Allow the children to run freely along the track. We would strongly advise adult supervision at first, with special emphasis on how important it is to stay on the track at all times. Try a follow-my-leader exercise with a small group of children following you while you vary both arm and leg movements. Stopping and starting activities can then be introduced by using the stations in a variety of ways. Use the children's names, for example, 'The train has now arrived at Stacey's station' whereupon Stacey gets off the train and waits at the stop until the train comes back for her. Alternatively the stops can be used as a signal for specific body movements. For example, 'We are coming to Jump Junction' when everyone begins to jump, or 'The train is arriving at Hopping Halt', when everyone starts to hop.

Follow-up

The children could extend these activities with a toy train set in the classroom. They can name their own stations and use cards to show the required movements at each stop.

Swallow the bean-bag

Objective
To develop accuracy in throwing skills by encouraging children to aim at a specific target.

What you need
Paints, brushes, a brick wall, bean-bags, buckets, hoops.

What to do
Paint the outline of a giant's head on a brick wall in the outside play area. The giant should have a wide open mouth, displaying large tonsils. He should be comical rather than gruesome, so as not to frighten young children.

Ask the children to practise throwing bean-bags at a given target, such as buckets or hoops arranged in an area of the playground. Young children usually find it easier to throw downwards at first, so just getting the children to throw the bean-bag aganst the wall will often be a major step forward. However, the giant's head will be a great incentive for this skill. The target can be used to encourage children to acquire increasingly demanding skills.
● Ask the children to hit the giant anywhere on his head with the bean-bag.
● Ask them to try to get the bean-bag into the giant's mouth.
● Introduce a scoring system such as giving one point if the bean-bag goes into his mouth, and two points if the children can hit his tonsils.

Follow-up
The final development can be a good introduction to various simple scoring games, when the children will be required to use additional skills to calculate their scores.

It's a goal!

Objective
To introduce the children to the ball control skills required to play established games.

What you need
Paint and a brush, an outdoor wall, a netball hoop, brackets, soft sponge balls, plastic cones, a whistle.

What to do
Arrange to have a football goal-post painted on a wall in the playground, preferably away from windows, and a netball hoop attached to low-level brackets on a similar wall, so that it is detachable and can be brought into the classroom for safe keeping.

Liaise with junior games teachers to arrange to take small groups of children along to observe older children's games sessions for a short time. This will serve as an excellent motivation for this activity.

Before introducing the children to the goal-posts and netball hoops, allow them to experiment freely with kicking and throwing soft sponge balls. Set out some plastic cones so that the footballers can practise their dribbling skills.

When the children are fairly confident at handling the balls, allow them to practise their shooting techniques. Encourage them to keep score and nominate a referee, providing her with a whistle to blow when a goal is scored.

The planet suite

Objective
To provide a simple but permanent environment for fantasy role-play.

What you need
Paint and a brush, cardboard boxes, masks, plastic lemonade bottles, toy cars, foil, card.

What to do
Paint an outline of a rocket ship on the playground with blast-off numbers (5, 4, 3, 2, 1, 0) in clouds of smoke coming from its tail end. Arrange painted planets

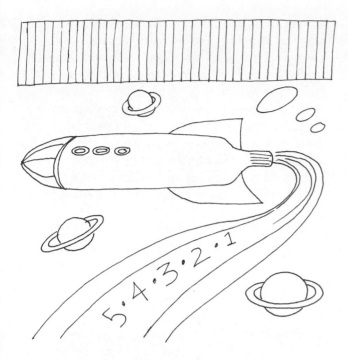

in orbit around the rocket. Because the space scene is painted outside, extra opportunities for movement between planets and rocket can be provided. This setting is very popular with young children, as many popular television programmes, books and comics use a space location.

Stimulate fantasy play with a collection of home-made space helmets (cardboard boxes), monster masks and oxygen tanks (empty plastic lemonade bottles). Space buggies could also be created by decorating toy cars or bikes with foil and card.

Children are usually very creative in inventing space monster plots and stories about journeys to the moon. Number counting can also be practised; encourage the children to count down for blast-off each time they use the rocket or space buggies.

Follow-up
Children greatly enjoy making robots and space creatures from junk. These can make a striking display when arranged on a plaster or foil lunar base board.

Down by the riverside

Objective
To create a role play situation which can be linked to real experiences.

What you need
Paint and a brush, a visit to a stream, river or canal, construction bricks, planks of wood, cardboard boxes or plastic storage boxes.

What to do
Paint on the playground an outline of a winding river, adding bushes and grass dotted around for authenticity. Sets of stepping stones can also be painted to create crossing points on the river.

Introduce the activity by organising a trip to a local stream, river or canal. This will provide an excellent discussion point to begin your role-play about the riverside. It also provides a perfect opportunity to discuss water safety and the dangers of playing unsupervised near water.

Extend the fantasy play in any of the following ways.
• Adapt the stepping stones to form triangle steps, square steps or circle steps. Alternatively, paint them in sequence patterns.
• Introduce technology by asking the children to design and build a bridge to cross the river, using large construction bricks and planks of wood.
• Let the children use cardboard boxes or plastic storage boxes as boats to stimulate the role-play.

Follow-up
The children might enjoy planning and making a picnic to enjoy by the river. A simple assortment of sandwiches and biscuits would create a realistic extension to the fantasy play.

Prepare the children for the fantasy play by reading lots of fairy stories involving magical happenings and magic spells. Help the children to plan a story of their own which would be suitable to act out in the designated outdoor play area. Encourage them to think of ingredients for a magic spell and provide them with a 'cauldron' (a large round casserole dish) and a 'magic wand' (shiny paper rolled into a tube and held in place with adhesive tape).

The children's originality will probably be short-lived in this particular role-play as they will quickly revert to realistic play situations with which they feel more comfortable. However, we feel that we must encourage the children to play imaginatively and creatively whenever possible in order to develop their artistic talents for story planning and interpretation.

The enchanted wood

Objective
To provide a stimulating, magical environment where the children can create fantasy situations.

What you need
Paints and a brush, a selection of clothes to stimulate appropriate fantasy play such as a cardboard crown, cloaks, gauzy fabric wings and wizard hats, a selection of fairy stories, a large round casserole dish, shiny paper, adhesive tape.

What to do
On an outside wall, paint outlines of trees, flowers and toadstools. These can be accompanied by cartoon-type butterflies and other fantasy creepy-crawlies.

Green fingers

Chapter nine

Establishing a school garden is extremely exciting and rewarding. It does not have to occupy a large area of land, and neither need it require back-breaking upkeep. A small patch of lawn with easily reached borders is more than sufficient. We were extremely lucky in acquiring all our small gardening tools from the local petrol station using gift vouchers issued with petrol sales. Many of the parents donated their vouchers and the school was able to create a large central store of trowels and forks.

If a garden is impractical, plants and shrubs can easily be grown in tubs and troughs around the playground. As well as looking attractive, they are an invaluable teaching resource.

One of the greatest drawbacks in growing seeds and bulbs is that it is a very slow process. Children soon become bored and lose interest when developments do not occur quickly. Aim to use seeds which germinate quickly, or young established plants bought from a garden centre. Children enjoy the responsibility of caring for other living things and soon become aware that all living things need certain conditions and food to ensure healthy growth.

Children who live in homes without a garden often show a particular fascination with growing things and delight in discovering root formations and buds. Many children in our school were amazed to see that potatoes actually grew beneath a green plant and were not manufactured in plastic bags on the supermarket shelf!

Cress names

Objective
To investigate the germination of seeds and to demonstrate that plants need water for healthy growth.

What you need
Mustard and cress seeds, shallow plastic trays, blotting paper, scissors, bread, butter.

What to do
Cut the blotting paper into interesting shapes. These can be fish, flower or star shapes, or any other which would be relevant to your work in the classroom. A particular favourite in our school is to cut out the initial letter of each child's name.

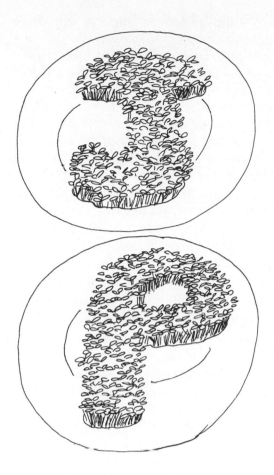

The same but different

Objective

To encourage the children to note similarities between flowers whilst also observing their differences.

What you need

A garden border or a collection of large pots, some small plant pots or troughs, sunflower and marigold seeds, gardening tools.

What to do

Let the children handle the seeds and examine them closely. Point out how the shiny striped cases of the sunflower seeds contrast with the fluffy, parachute type seeds of the marigolds. Let the children plant the seeds, making sure they understand the need for careful watering throughout the germination time. When

Place the blotting paper in shallow trays and thoroughly soak it with water. Once the blotting paper has absorbed all the water it can, pour off the excess. Sprinkle the seeds over the damp paper surface as evenly as possible. Place some trays outside and keep others indoors for the children to observe the germination process. Tell the children that they must not let the blotting paper dry out, and encourage them to make regular comparisons between the outside and inside seeds.

The children will be delighted to see their initials once the seedlings have grown, and will also enjoy cutting the cress and making sandwiches with it.

The children will learn from this activity that seeds need warmth and moisture to aid the germination and growth cycle.

the flowers begin to grow, the changes will be very dramatic. The children will be quite surprised by the rate of growth in the sunflower especially. Encourage the children to compare these two yellow flowers, which both have green stems, leaves, roots and yellow petals but also have such an outstanding difference in size.

Follow-up

If the flowers are allowed to die off naturally, the children can collect the seeds. This can be another fascinating learning experience related to the growth cycle of a plant. The sunflower seeds can supplement the feeding of school pets. Our hamsters and guinea pigs feasted for weeks on our crop!

In a dark, dark, cupboard

Objective

To introduce the children to flower bulbs and to highlight the differences between bulbs and seeds.

What you need

An assortment of bulbs such as crocus, hyacinth, daffodil, tulip and snowdrop, pots, bulb fibre, a glass bulb pot or jam jar, a cupboard, beakers, drinking straws.

What to do

Growing bulbs indoors is a firm classroom favourite, but it is important that the children realise the conditions necessary for the bulbs to grow.

Let the children grow bulbs in water, in pots of bulb fibre and in the garden. Show them how the bulbs will grow well in a cold dark cupboard, but explain that they should be moved into the light once the green shoots are fairly well developed. Discuss the bulbs that are grown in water and point out how the roots suck up water. Let the children imitate this process by sucking up water from a beaker through several drinking straws at once. Explain that the hyacinths can grow in water because they have all the necessary food stored in the bulb.

Encourage the children to observe the differences between bulbs grown outside and those grown indoors. They will be interested to observe that the blooms grown indoors are often dead and gone before the green shoots appear in the garden. Ask them why they think this might be.

Follow-up

If plants such as celery or white carnations are placed in a strong solution of food dye and water, the children can see how the liquid is drawn up into them and observe the coloured celery ridges and carnation petals which result.

Miniature gardens

Objective
To plan and design a garden on a small model scale.

What you need
Seed trays, compost, newspaper, pebbles and larger stones, a selection of small, shallow rooted plants (such as miniature sedum and London pride, aubrietia, saxifrage, alpines and any rock garden plants), mosses, LEGO bricks, small foil dishes.

What to do
Ask the children what they would expect to find in a typical garden. Encourage them to use words such as lawn, flower beds, paths, rockeries and garden pools. Organise a walk along some local residential streets specifically to look at gardens. Ask some parents who live nearby whether you could bring the children to look round their gardens. Encourage the children to look out for different kinds of flowers, trees, garden ornaments, etc.

Let the children work together to design and make their own miniature gardens. Ask them to line seed trays with

newspaper before filling them with compost. Explain that this helps to retain the water. Let them use moss as a lawn and show them how to plant small shallow plants. They can use pebbles to make rockeries and small foil dishes as garden ponds.

Our children were very imaginative in this work and asked to borrow the LEGO to make garden swings, benches and gnomes to go in their gardens. The plants grew all year and the children cared for them quite meticulously.

Pressed flowers

Objective
To introduce the children to the technique of preserving flowers by drying and pressing them.

What you need
A commercial flower press or some heavy books, blotting paper, some fresh garden or wild flowers.

What to do
Let the children explore the school garden or their own gardens to collect flower heads. They will greatly enjoy being suddenly positively encouraged to pick flowers as a pleasant change from being told not to do so! Once a substantial collection has been made, ask the children to press their flowers. This must be done before the blooms begin to wilt and become discoloured. It is important at this stage to sort through the flowers and discard any which are particularly thick and bulky. These can either be separated into individual petals for pressing or else discarded. The flowers which are most successful when pressed are sweet peas, primroses,

and encourage them to look at the trees. Children are usually fascinated by the size of the tree roots (which are often exposed in large trees) and the height of the trees. Obvious labelling discussions can take place about trunk, branch, leaf, bark, and so on, but also draw the children's attention to the shape of the tree. For example, point out how the shape of a conifer is very different from that of an oak tree. Use a simple tree guide book to help you identify trees from their shapes as well as their leaves. Encourage the children to collect a variety of fallen leaves. Back in the classroom, ask the children to examine the leaves closely and try to classify them. Get them to look closely at details such as veins and different colours. The differences are usually very obvious.

Show the children some bonsai trees or miniature conifers. These will stimulate great interest.

buttercups and others with delicate heads. To quicken the pressing process, lay the flowers between sheets of blotting paper which help absorb the moisture. The flowers should be ready after two weeks.

Follow-up
There are all kinds of art work to be done with the dried, pressed flowers. They make excellent bookmarks and cards but are very delicate to work with. The children must be guided to apply the adhesive to the paper or card and then fix the flower to the sticky surface.

Tree shapes

Objective
To raise the children's awareness of tree and leaf shapes.

What you need
A book about trees, bonsai trees or miniature conifers.

What to do
Take the children for a walk outside in the school grounds on a fine autumn day

Follow-up
The children could do rubbings of the leaves with wax crayons. These will look particularly effective if they are then washed over with a water-based ink such as Brusho.

A rock garden

Objective
To develop aesthetic awareness and encourage children to make attractive arrangements of plants and rocks.

What you need
A collection of rocks with interesting colour and texture contrasts (good examples would be rainwashed limestone, sandstone, granite, slate or marble), varnish, soil, a selection of suitable rockery plants such as aubrietia, whiterock, alpines and saxifrage, gardening tools.

What to do
Designate a small area of your school garden to create a rockery. Just one example of each type of rock or stone would be sufficient to draw the children's attention to the fact that not all rocks and stones are the same. Encourage the children to touch the rocks and feel both their coldness and their texture, and look at details such as colour and shape. Varnish the slate before placing it in the rockery as this highlights the colours even more.

A large amount of soil will need to be spread and shaped to make the rockery, and then the children can be involved in choosing positions for the rocks.

Let the children plant the rockery plants around the rocks. Point out any possible colour clashes and pleasant foliage contrasts.

Follow-up
The children will love to watch the plants grow and spread, filling in the spaces between the rocks. If a large area is available for the rockery, perhaps stepping stones could be positioned through the rocks, so the children can walk through the rock garden taking a closer look at the plants.

A smelly garden

Objective

To show the children that plants not only look different, but also have quite distinctive smells.

What you need

A selection of growing herbs and plants with fairly strong smells (such as lavender, mint, lemon balm, thyme, sage and chives), an area of garden or troughs and large pots, gardening tools, potting compost.

What to do

If you do not have an area of open ground which you could transform into a smelly garden, large plant pots or troughs would suffice. The suggested plants can be bought at most good garden centres. If you are transplanting them into open ground it is important that they are very near the edge of a path or the playground, as the children must be able to reach them quite easily in order to smell their scent.

Prepare the ground or pots in advance, then let the children plant the herbs. Make sure they tend them over the following weeks while the roots are becoming established.

Let the children smell the plants by sniffing them directly. Show them how if they rub the leaves between their fingers, the odours are released in an even stronger form, making their hands and fingers smell. Encourage them to try to describe the various smells.

Follow-up

• The children could make their own smelly flowers by covering a cotton wool ball with fabric and then applying scented oil. These can be attached as centres to pre-painted flowers.
• Some of the plants from the smelly garden are edible. The chives can be chopped and eaten with cheese and the mint is pleasant when a leaf or two is added to cold lemonade.

Taking care

Chapter ten

Raising children's awareness of the environment and the need to care for the earth is a topical issue of great importance. Most young children have a certain knowledge of 'green' issues and show a great concern about conservation.

Naturally, the degree to which these topics can be investigated will be determined by the children's understanding and development. Nevertheless, a foundation can be developed in the early years, upon which responsibility and a desire to care for the environment can be built later.

Young children take a natural delight in exploring their surroundings, and if we can introduce them to the aesthetic qualities of nature now, the appreciation and wonderment may last and contribute to the preservation of nature's beauty in the future.

The colours of nature

Objective
To develop in children an aesthetic appreciation of their natural surroundings.

What you need
Paint colour charts, paint, palettes, brushes, paper.

What to do
Before the activity, show the children some paint colour charts and point out how the colours vary. Explain that this is dependent upon different quantities of

various colours being mixed together. Let the children experiment with colour mixing for themselves.

Ask the children to mix as many shades of brown and green as possible and paint blobs of each colour on to a piece of paper to make their own colour chart. Once the colour charts are dry, let the children take them outside on a 'colour-matching nature walk'. Encourage the children to find natural things to match the shades they have made as closely as possible, by looking at the trees, plants, soil and stones.

This exercise should make the children aware of the beautiful shades and contrasts of colour which nature provides. It will also serve as an introduction to further work on the environment, if you emphasise how important it is to preserve and care for our surroundings.

Follow-up
The children can do leaf prints or paint their own 'free expression' pictures of what they found on the walk using the shades of paint they have mixed.

Rubbish hunt

Objective
To introduce the children to the concept of caring for the environment by keeping it litter-free.

What you need
Plastic or rubber gloves, plastic bags, newspapers, empty cardboard boxes.

What to do
Take the children for a litter hunt around the playground and in the local streets. Make sure that the children wear

protective gloves. Provide large plastic bags in which they can collect litter. While they do this, ask the children where the rubbish ought to have been placed and who they think may have dropped it. Our children were amazed at how much litter there was once it was collected, and they became quite concerned about the problem. This prompted them to design posters and send a letter to our local council asking for litter bins to be provided outside the school. To our delight, the council agreed and soon fixed bins to the railings.

Bring the litter into the playground and lay it out on sheets of newspaper so that the children can sort it, again wearing protective gloves. Use cardboard boxes to categorise the rubbish into paper and cardboard, glass, metal, plastic, wood and food. Ask the children which rubbish they think is dangerous. Encourage them to think about the possible damage sharp objects and glass could do to animals, and how rotten food can attract vermin and insects.

Ask the children how they think the litter could be disposed of safely. Encourage them to consider which items could be recycled and which are biodegradable.

Follow-up
The children could make junk pictures using clean 'rubbish' such as empty boxes, wool and scraps of cloth. These are very effective when they are colour co-ordinated, with one picture for red junk, one for yellow junk, and so on.

Digging deep

Objective
To raise the children's awareness about the decomposition of rubbish.

What you need
Garden spades, assorted rubbish, plastic gloves, lolly sticks, paper, pencils.

What to do
Children need to be made aware that most of our refuse is taken to tips, where it is eventually covered with earth to hide its unsightliness. Ask the children to predict what they think will happen to various pieces of rubbish once they have been buried.

Set up a simple experiment to test these predictions. Let the children dig holes in damp ground and bury the rubbish. Provide a variety of rubbish which will and will not decompose, such as vegetable matter, paper, plastic and tin. Let the children cover these with earth and mark them with lolly sticks and labels illustrating the buried item. Leave the items for at least two weeks and then dig them up to see what has happened.

The paper and food items should show signs of decomposing, but the plastic will not. The children might identify the discolouring on the tins as rust. We would recommend that the teacher digs up the rubbish, as it is a health hazard, especially the food.

Food for thought

Objective
To increase the children's awareness of the interdependence of nature.

What you need
Safety pins, string, thin card, felt-tipped pens.

What to do
Before the activity, prepare pictures of the following things on thin card and attach them to safety pins to make badges:
- a bird;
- a worm;
- a leaf;
- an aphid;
- a ladybird.

Let the children wear the badges and ask them to stand in a circle in the outdoor play area. Discuss the pictures and involve the children in a discussion about the links between them. Give the child with the ladybird picture a ball of string and ask him to hold on to the end and pass on the ball. As the string unravels it should illustrate the linking process as follows: the ladybird eats the aphid . . . the aphid eats the leaf . . . the leaf decomposes into soil . . . the soil is eaten by the worm . . . the worm is eaten by the bird.

The result will be a linked network made from one piece of string and a practical demonstration for the children of the interdependence of nature. The children can be shown that if one of the components is removed, the whole network could collapse. Each is as important as the next, with a significant role to play in the natural world.

Follow-up
The children could go on a nature hunt to look for evidence of the activities which they have demonstrated, such as nibbled leaves, birds looking for worms and decaying leaves in the soil.

Dirty work

Objective
To encourage the children to investigate the composition of soil and its properties.

What you need
Trowels, buckets, paper, yoghurt pots with a series of holes made in the bottom, plastic containers, watering can.

What to do
Ask the children what they think they might find in the soil. Then allow them to go outside to gather samples from

various locations such as a flower border, under the grass or under a tree. Explain that different samples must be kept in different buckets. Encourage the children to look for the remains of plant life, stones or even living creatures, but emphasise the fact that the latter should be returned to the soil as soon as possible.

Encourage the children to examine the soil samples closely. Do the samples all look and feel the same? Let them rub the different soil samples on to paper to see if they leave the same sort of mark.

Lead the children into a discussion about the uses of soil. Growth of plants will be the immediate answer. Develop this into an activity to see whether the various samples of soil will retain water to enable plants to grow. Point out that too much water can kill a plant just as easily as too little. Make holes in the bottom of some yoghurt pots. Put samples of soil in the yoghurt pots, then place the pots inside plastic containers. Pour measured amounts of water over each soil sample and let the children investigate the draining properties of the soils by comparing the amounts of water which pass through.

Squeaky clean

Objective
To introduce the concept of caring for ourselves.

What you need
Magnifying glasses, warm and cold water, various kinds of soap.

What to do
After digging in the garden, encourage the children to look closely at the dirt on their hands through a magnifying glass. This will highlight how the grime collects in the creases of skin and in its pores. Let the children experiment outside with bowls of warm and cold water and with solid and liquid soap to see which is the most effective way of cleaning their hands.

Arrange the bowls in a specific order and let the children do a progressive series of handwashes, examining them with a magnifying glass after each wash. An experiment with bowl 1 containing cold water, bowl 2 containing warm water, bowl 3 containing cold water and soap, then finally bowl 4 containing warm water and soap should achieve the desired results.

Looking down on things, see page 42